ROBERT BRIDGES

T0346175

# ROBERT BRIDGES

*BY*

## G. S. GORDON

*The Rede Lecture, 1931*

*Cambridge*
*at the University Press*
*1946*

# CAMBRIDGE
## UNIVERSITY PRESS

University Printing House, Cambridge CB2 8BS, United Kingdom

Published in the United States of America by Cambridge University Press, New York

Cambridge University Press is part of the University of Cambridge.

It furthers the University's mission by disseminating knowledge in the pursuit of education, learning and research at the highest international levels of excellence.

www.cambridge.org
Information on this title: www.cambridge.org/9781107634558

© Cambridge University Press 1946

First published 1946
Re-issued 2014

*A catalogue record for this publication is available from the British Library*

ISBN 978-1-107-63455-8 Paperback

# NOTE

Like many others, this essay owes its fifteen years' sequestration to my husband's repugnance to seeing himself in print. A year after the delivery of the Rede Lecture he wrote to a friend: 'The lecture has lain in a drawer since this time last year: I wish I could overcome that feeling of disgust which overtakes me when I have written anything. It must be from some such feeling that animals eat their young.'

I have felt it to be my duty to rescue the lecture from the drawer, and prepare it for the Cambridge University Press.

MARY GORDON

*May 1946*

# ROBERT BRIDGES

LET me begin by acknowledging the honour which the University of Cambridge has done me in permitting my name to figure among its officers of the year as Sir Robert Rede's Lecturer. Of the life and merits of the founder, about whom, on my appointment, I piously informed myself, I will say only that I found his distinguished career as a Tudor Justice less immediately interesting, and also less innocent, than his membership of what once was Buckingham College, and is now, as I must think, more happily called Magdalene. The notable list of my predecessors in this Lectureship is a more serious matter, and a ground for complacency rather to Cambridge than to me. I come, besides, from another place. But I hope that, where I fail, my theme may save me. For I have chosen to speak of one of the noblest figures of our time, of a poet and man of letters who belonged to England, indeed, but in whom Oxford had a special share, and who honoured me in his last years with his friendship.

The death nine months ago of Robert Bridges, however deeply we may grudge it, coming when it did, in his 86th year, in the full glow of a last magnificent accomplishment, must be counted happy. His friends had observed, as the *Testament of Beauty* neared completion, a growing anxiety to reach the end, and make up his account at once with art and nature. Habitual as its speculations had become to him, and easily as it moves in its 'loose Alexandrines', now like a hale old countryman in clouted shoon, now like some pacing patriarch, so sustained a performance must have tried a younger man, and it seems that he feared some sudden failure of strength. As it proved, he not only finished the *Testament*, but lived to revise it, and to enjoy unaffectedly, as indeed he enjoyed everything, the glow of a public approbation so warm and home-felt that even his memory could not have supplied a modern parallel. The barrier of reserve between a nation accustomed to more accommodating officials and a Laureate who was first of all a private gentleman broke down before the conjunction of this unexpected masterpiece and an 85th birthday. One of his chief satisfactions was in the sale of the poem, for he had always wished, and now more than ever, to be read.

It was difficult to believe, on meeting Mr Bridges, so easily did he breathe our biting modern air, that he was born in the first decade of the reign of Queen Victoria, and learned his letters in the Laureateship of Wordsworth. He was so frankly and vitally there before you, with such challenge in voice and eye, and in the whole splendid length of him, shaggy-crowned, such lounging and half-arrogant power. Even that atmosphere which lay about him as of some ampler, more leisured, and now vanished age, hardly prepared one for the discovery that he had been familiar as a child with the sight of the Great Duke (a valued memory), and had watched, as a boy of ten, from a Walmer garden, the departure of Napier's fleet for the Baltic under the new power of steam—in those days when first was seen

low and black<br>Beside the full-rigg'd mast the strange smoke-stack.

There must have been much that he could tell about the great Victorians and their ways, but somehow one did not think to ask him. There was never a man less built for the part of mumbling ancestor. His talk was not of bygones, but of present, future, or eternal things: his work or yours, what the scientists or psychologists were doing, or the younger poets, what wireless *will* do, or if the sun shone and nature luxuriated, the life of birds and flowers, perhaps, or the principles of beauty and rightness in the conduct and the arts of man.

If it was difficult to make a Nestor of Mr Bridges, quite another difficulty awaits the critically minded who cannot know him and have yet to read him. Posterity, it is certain, encountering his last and greatest work, will be puzzled to understand, without much more knowledge than is yet prepared for it, how a man of his generation, however favoured by longevity, should have presented to what is almost the generation of his grandchildren, not only the finest but in many ways the most representative poem of our time. This is already indeed a puzzle to numerous readers of the present day, among them old adherents, contented quoters of his lyrics, who had thought until 1930 that they knew their Bridges.

The answer to such perplexities is biography, by which I mean that history of the spiritual and artistic life which is more especially the biography of poets. It is now a fashion to study intently the youth of great poets, and there is poetical reason for it. It is in those early years that the Delphic stamp is taken. It is now well recognized that in those once *unnoticed* years of youth and childhood—for, in their biographies, our ancestors hastened always to the grown man—a poet accumulates by far the greatest and most valuable portion of the natural riches on which he is to draw for life. Bridges himself dwells on this. 'That children have an innate love of Beauty is undeniable. . . . While the intellectual faculty is still dormant, spiritual things are to children as music is, which a child readily absorbs, without thought, although a full-grown man, if he has lacked that happy initiation, can scarcely by grammar come at the elements.' In his scheme of life, indeed, as his *Testament* has revealed, he traces the hopes and prospects of mankind to the natural desire, only gradually relaxed and never wholly lost, for what is beautiful and good, which may be seen in the wondering eyes of children, and by Christian symbol, in the face of the young Christ.

The life of Robert Bridges is in neither its inner nor its outer aspects other than very imperfectly known to the present generation. This is the fate, no doubt, of men who outlive their contemporaries, and lead, besides, as Bridges did, an intensely private life. It was a fate, I may add, which he regarded with equanimity. He had hoped, or so I fancy, that he had settled with that, and closed the door on further publicity, when he fused all the thought and art and passion of his long life in the *Testament of Beauty*. There was his last confession, his sifted and essential autobiography. The effect of the poem, if I may judge by various signs, has, in fact, been just the contrary. It has brought the world at last acquainted with his life, but in such a manner that it must know more. Had he continued, as once seemed likely, to be regarded and esteemed as in the main a lyric poet, the public, no doubt, would have borne its ignorance with unconcern. But the *Testament* has changed all that; and because it is so plainly the magnificent echo of a splendid nature and the last message of a complete life, the public which has been thumbing the unexpected gospel, looks naturally for elucidation, and above all for a life of the apostle. He himself, I must think unfortunately, took another view. There was to be no official or authorized life: on that he was clear and indeed insistent. Yet somehow, by someone, from material thus necessarily imperfect, it will be done.

It is on the youth of Robert Bridges that most has been revealed to us: much may be gathered from his memoirs of others, and these and similar indications will, no doubt, sometime be faithfully gathered together. In outline the biographical portrait is clear enough. He comes before us first as a boy at Eton, and happy there; to the end it is 'the beloved school'; and his Founder's Day Ode is not only the best of Eton Odes, which is saying much, but one of the best of his poems, which is saying more. He was almost *formed*, I should say, at Eton, so well it suited him, and by the time he went to Oxford had taken his mould. Fortune had been kind to him— and seldom through life relented in this benevolence —endowing him with every handsomeness of mind and body, and with the means, moreover, of future leisure. He was athlete, musician, and scholar; had the friends he wished, and had them without effort; and like many serious lads, before and since, believed himself destined for the Church. He passed to Oxford, which shared henceforth with Eton in his institutional affections; read widely and philosophically; was the best stroke of his year; and, wiser than some of his Victorian predecessors in the Laureateship, decided that even a poet should have a profession. His choice was masterly, for, being a poet, he chose science. The rest may be briefly told. After some travel in Egypt, Syria and later in Germany, he went to St Bartholomew's Hospital and became a doctor, practised for ten years, and latterly with distinction, and only then, at 38, left the hated town for poetry and a country life. In the 47 years which he had still to live he remained faithful to poetry and a country life. Some twenty of his quiet middle years were spent at Yattendon, where in 1884 he married Monica, daughter of his friend Alfred Waterhouse; the rest of his days at Chilswell, the house he had built on Boar's Hill, near Oxford.

He was in practice no party to that extremity of criticism which demands that poetry shall be read without reference to its authors. There are times for that; but it will always be true, as Bridges himself has said, that 'those who admire or love a poet's work are instinctively drawn to the *man*, and are eager to learn anything that may deepen their intimacy'. In one of those fragments of autobiography which inlay his memoirs of his early friends, he has noted the precise occasion when the attractions of literature first appeared to him. 'I was eleven years of age,' he says, 'in the lower school [at Eton], in the division called Sense, when I first read Ovid, and some elegies of his opened my eyes to Poetry.' Ovid in his time has opened many eyes, but not always to art. It was his command of his medium that won this schoolboy, and Bridges' natural bent for craftsmanship, for the *Art* of Poetry, became presently clear. It was brought home to him early by the different attitude of his young friend Dolben, who was a junior in the same House and, like Bridges, a furtive composer. '...we were mutually coy of exposing our secret productions, which were so antipathetically bad.' On the nature of this antipathy Mr Bridges has an important passage. 'Our instinctive attitudes towards poetry', he says, 'were very dissimilar, he regarded it from the emotional, and I from the artistic side; and he was thus of a much intenser poetic temperament than I, for when he began to write poetry he would never have written on any subject that did not deeply move him, nor would he attend to poetry unless it expressed his own emotions.... What had led me to poetry was the inexhaustible satisfaction of form, the magic of speech, lying as it seemed to me in the masterly control of the material: it was an art which I hoped to learn. An instinctive rightness was essential, but, given that, I did not suppose that the poet's emotions were in any way better than mine, nor mine than another's: and, though I should not at that time have put it in these words, I think that Dolben imagined poetic form to be the naïve outcome of peculiar personal emotion; just as one imagines in nature the universal mind conquering nature by the urgence of life,—as he himself describes it in his "Core":

> Poetry, the hand that wrings
> (Bruised albeit at the strings)
> Music from the soul of things.

There is a point in art where these two ways merge and unite, but in apprenticehood they are opposite approaches.'

This is a valuable statement and is the proper preface to any account of Mr Bridges' poetry. Dolben's assumption that emotional urgence will find or make its own form is the romantic, and also the amateur, view in all the arts, and can only be disproved by failure. Neither on this nor on one other point to which he draws attention did Bridges change. I mean his inability to suppose that the emotions of the poets he read were any better than his own, or his own than another's. Many years later, in his famous essay on Keats he reaffirms this:

'There must be thousands and thousands of persons alive at this moment in England, who, if they could only give poetic expression to those mysterious feelings with which they are moved in the presence of natural beauty, would be one and all of them greater poets than have ever yet been.' This is easily said, but Bridges meant it. What these thousands of people want, of course, is art; an art equal to that mystery. But their souls are right. No less than his respect for art is his faith in the human spirit, at whatever stage of articulation, and this was a tenet of his creed to the end. It is so declared in his last poem, and indeed is a necessity of its reasoning. I speak of it now because the thorough-paced artist, as Bridges was, has so seldom held this view. It is of a piece with his devout humanity.

The same Memoir of Dolben introduces us to Bridges at the age of 17, 'reading Shakespeare for the first time', and finding, what so many schoolmasters take no account of, that his imperfect understanding 'hindered neither my enjoyment nor admiration'. He was already deep in his favourite Milton—the First Book of *Paradise Lost* had dazed him with its grandeur—and he carried Keats about with him in his pocket. The eager Dolben tried to lure him to the new poetry and fashions of the day—to Mr and Mrs Browning, Tennyson, Ruskin and the rest: all then in their glory, for I am speaking of 1862. But already he was exhibiting his characteristic power of refusing the wrong diet, knowing instinctively that it *was* wrong, for *him*. Ruskin: No. Tennyson: the early lyrics—he had them by heart; but not, he was sure, *The Idylls of the King*. '...when I heard *The Idylls of the King* praised as if they were the final attainment of all poetry, then I drew into my shell, contented to think that I might be too stupid to understand, but that I could never expect as good a pleasure from following another's taste as I got from my own.' Yet he yielded to the vogue sufficiently to choose from the *Idylls* his speech on the 4th of June, 'wherewith I indulged', he says, 'the ears of his late majesty K. Edward VII on the year of his marriage; and I even purchased as gifts to my friends the fashionable volumes which I had never read through'. Dolben made a later attempt with *Enoch Arden*, just out in 1864. 'Are you not made happy by Tennyson's new volume? It was worth all one's long waiting and expectation indeed.' Bridges, however, had *not* been waiting, nor had he any considerable expectations from it. 'I remember reading it,' he says (in a sentence which stages him), 'without all Digby's enthusiasm, in the hot sun on a treeless cricket-field waiting for my innings.'

I dwell on these things because his life is so little

known and because in essentials he changed so little, because this schoolboy of 18 is so like the man I knew. He came to have some half a dozen languages at his command, and was a wide and intent but increasingly selective and capricious reader. There had so seldom been any reason why he should persevere with what he did not like, or open, indeed, at all, what failed to invite him. It was his one complaint against Mr W. P. Ker that he was so catholic, that not content with the appalling self-sacrifice of reading everything, he actually tried (could it be believed?) to *like* everything also—for something. When Mr Bridges had decided that Dryden, for example, had nothing that he wanted, it was no good speaking to him of Dryden's other abilities; he was done with Dryden. It is the difference between the reading of the scholar and the artist, even when the artist is a scholar: the mature artist, at any rate, reads not so much to enlarge his taste as to confirm or refine it. In the essay on Keats he has occasion to mention, as something generally known, the bad effect on that poet's work of the poetry of Leigh Hunt. He *makes* the statement; but a footnote assures us that he had not shared in Keats' defilement. 'I have not read Hunt's poems', he says; why should he? What enfeebled Keats he was not called on to endure. He was to meet, in later life, various reminders of his omissions. In 1916, addressing the Tredegar Cooperative Society, he confessed, at the risk of forfeiting their confidence, as he acknowledged, that Macaulay's *Essays*—one of the best-sellers of his boyhood—was still, at that date, practically a new book to him. He had found a volume of them that summer in a holiday cottage—'an inscription in it reminded', he says, 'how it had been won by its owner in a whist-drive'. He read it through, and was astonished to find Macaulay praising Shelley, and even in terms which he approved. For Browning, another urgent and elder contemporary, he had never cared, and the result is plainly seen in his famous war-time anthology. When asked why this famous poet, a sursum corda man, if ever there was one, should have been altogether omitted from *The Spirit of Man*, a volume intended to encourage, he truthfully replied, taking only the immediate question, that he supposed there wasn't a Browning in the house. This is English as well as aesthetic. I am reminded of a sentence in Professor Conington's edition of Virgil. 'The editions of the classics to which I have referred', he says, 'have been in general the best and latest, when my library happened to contain them.' This perfectly intelligible English standpoint, that an Englishman is a private gentleman and householder *first*, and an editor or anthologist afterwards, is one that our foreign neighbours will never understand.

The result of this perfect freedom on Mr Bridges' taste and mind has been best described by his friend Sir Walter Raleigh—Letter to Lady Elcho, October, 1912:

'Robert Bridges has just been in on the way down the hill. He is delightfully grumpy. He mentions thing after thing which is commonly believed and says that of course it's not so. He's always right. His intellect has been so completely self-indulged that it now can't understand rubbish. He has never obeyed anyone or adapted himself to anyone, so he's as clear as crystal, and can't do with fogs. He brought with him', he goes on, 'a nice bright-eyed girl, or child, who hung on his words and thought ineffable things which played over her face like a little breeze, while we, the Old and Horny, did the talking.

'What fun it would be if children had the power of speech!'

This is Bridges as he was.

It may have struck you—it struck many who knew Bridges—how little of all this masculine character, this brusqueness, this humorous self-will, is to be found in the poetry which he spent most of his life producing; the poetry by which he gradually and rightly became famous, and by which he is best known even now. What struck one about much of his earlier verse—the beautiful lyrics, odes and sonnets—was not only the perfection of their form and keeping, the exquisite insight of their observation, and the purity of their moods, but—how much of himself, of the man one knew,—of the man who at last spoke out in the *Testament of Beauty*—he had contrived to keep out of them. Even his friends would remark that he was too constantly aware that the Muses are maidens. There was something in the charge. I have here the 1873 volume: of the 52 poems which it contained only 18 were reprinted: and for the most part with good reason. But there are two poems which I claim to rescue here and now, the first and the last, from their author's delicacy.

> Her eye saw, her eye stumbled:
>   Her fingers spread and touched it:
> It was so ripe it tumbled
>   Off in her hand, that clutched it.

She raised it up to smell it:
  Her jealous tongue ran o'er it:
Ere the thought rose to quell it,
  Her keen teeth closed and tore it.

There, as she stood in wonder,
  And smacked the flavour fruity,
She scanned it o'er and under,
  And marvelled at its beauty.

'It's fair,' she said, 'and fairest
  Just where the sun's rays strike it;
The taste's the strangest, rarest;
  It's bitter, but I like it.'

---

To man she brought it, bitten,
  She brought it, she the woman,
The fruit, of which 'tis written
  The eating should undo man.

'Taste, taste!' she cried, 'thou starvest;
  Eat as I ate, nor fear it,
For of all the garden's harvest
  There's nothing like or near it.

'Fair to the eyes, and fairest
  Just where the sun's rays strike it:
But oh! the taste's the rarest,
  It's bitter, but thou'lt like it.'

---

He took the fruit she gave him,
  Took it for pain or pleasure:
There was no help could save him,
  Her measure was his measure.

Through her teeth's print, the door of it,
  He sent his own in after;
He ate rind, flesh, and core of it,
  And burst out into laughter.

''Tis fair,' he cried, 'and fairest
  Just where the sun's rays strike it:
The taste's the strangest, rarest,
  It's bitter, and I like it.'

Should it be saved? Bridges would evidently not allow this poem, either as frivolous, or too outspoken, to spoil the neighbourhood of his purer Muse.

The second is dated 1869: it also was published in the 1873 volume.

### EPITAPH ON A GENTLEMAN OF THE CHAPEL ROYAL

Old Thunder...s is dead, we weep for that,
He sings for aye his lowest note, B flat.
Unpursed his mouth, empty his mighty chest,
His run is o'er, and none may bar his rest.
We hope he is not d—d, for if he be
He's on the wrong side of the middle sea.

Nay we are sure if weighed he will not fail
Against the Devil to run down the scale;
While even three-throated Cerberus must retreat
From one that bellows from his sixteen feet:
Or should he meet with Peter at the door,
He'll seize the proper key as heretofore,
And by an easy turn he'll quickly come
From common time straight to *ad libitum*.
There in the equal temperament of Heaven,
Sharps, crotchets, accidentals, all forgiven,
He'll find his place directly, and perspire
Among the bases of the Elysian quire.
   Fear, dwellers on the Earth, this acquisition
To the divine etherial ammunition;
A thunder is let loose, a very wonder
Of earthborn, pitiless, Titanic thunder:
We who remain below and hear his roar
Must kneel and tremble where we laughed before.

Bridges' answers to the charge cannot well be resisted. His first answer was that the orthodox forms, in which he excelled, did not admit of such matter. His second and final answer was the *Testament of Beauty*.

I had thought at one time of making this poem the principal subject of my lecture, and even to the end the choice was tempting, so noble are its vistas of the spirit, so rich its landscapes, so whimsical and affectionate its humours. The whole man is there as nowhere else in all his writings. But the months have passed; the poem has been discussed; no literary society but has this title on its programme; it has even attained, within less than a year of publication, in a recent volume of annotations, the languorous honours of a classic. I propose, therefore, to answer in terms of it the exception that I myself used to take to Bridges' restriction of his moods, and to answer also the question, why he did not write the *Testament* sooner. When the *Testament of Beauty* appeared in 1930 he had been publishing poetry for 57 years. For a leisured man with so ripe a message it was a long time to wait. The proper person to answer these questions, I am well aware, was Mr Bridges, and I believe that he would have been willing to answer them, so far as he has not already answered them in print. But asking questions, as Dr Johnson said, is not a mode of conversation among gentlemen, and that opportunity for prying has gone. It will be something if I can reduce the naïve surprise with which the *Testament* was received, and is still, I observe, regarded by many readers who thought they knew Bridges' work; not the common surprise that Bridges should have written it in his eighties, but surprise that it should have been written by Bridges at all. Nor is the riddle much resolved by the authentic intelligence that the *Testament of Beauty* owes nothing, as composition, to the slow garnering of years, but was an entirely fresh work, tentatively begun in 1926. Between the *Testament of Beauty* and that poetry of studied ode and delicately silvered lyric by which Mr Bridges made his name and entered for ever the anthologies, the contrast, indeed, is striking at almost every point: as if Chaucer, abandoning the acquired metres of culture and his Legends of Good Women, should have startled Court and Custom House with 'In a somer seson' and that May-morning slumber on Malvern Hills. Listen to these lines from the *Testament of Beauty*:

'Twas late in my long journey, when I had clomb to where
the path was narrowing and the company few,
a glow of childlike wonder enthral'd me, as if my sense
had come to a new birth purified, my mind enrapt
re-awakening to a fresh initiation of life;
with like surprise of joy as any man may know
who rambling wide hath turn'd, resting on some hill-top
to view the plain he has left, and see'th it now out-spredd
mapp'd at his feet, a landscape so by beauty estranged
he scarce will ken familiar haunts, nor his own home,
maybe, where far it lieth, small as a faded thought.

To the large number of readers whose only idea of Mr Bridges was drawn from *The Growth of Love* and some of the shorter Poems, from

> 'My lady pleases me and I please her;
> This know we both.....'

or

> 'I have loved flowers that fade'

the new style, quite apart from its accompanying swarm of thought, seemed the work of some other and more spatulous hand. But these were superficial impressions. The loose and roomy metre of the *Testament* is, in fact, the last fruit of prosodic investigation, of a series of experiments carried on by the poet with perfect frankness for many years, and to that, and that alone, we owe that the poem was ever written. This is not the usual order in the genesis of poetry, but it was Bridges' order. Had he failed to discover the metre of the *Testament*, I will not say that he would never have written his philosophy. He spoke often of doing so, sometimes, in despair, of doing it in prose. I have noticed, indeed, that his Broadcast Lecture on Poetry, given in 1929, is an advance statement of the principles of his poem. But he would not have written the *Testament of Beauty*.

That preoccupation with form which determined the natal chances of his last poem was a characteristic of Mr Bridges all his life, and one of his principal later investigations, pursued even through the morass of quantitative hexameters, was to find a form of verse looselimbed enough, and sufficiently capacious and accommodating to admit humour and philosophy, and generally the rambling expatiations of the mind. From 1903, when he published his poems in Classical Prosody, to 1921, when he wrote *Poor Poll* and its companion pieces, he was still searching for the metre in which the *Testament* is composed. It is satisfactory to see one shaft at any rate of these prosodic tunnellings, on which he was thought to waste his time, emerge in this poem into the sunlight and the approving eye of day. I believe, as he did, that his Neo-Miltonics (if only they might be called by another name!) have a great future before them in English poetry.

I cannot omit to recommend to you, as an adjunct to his poetry, Mr Bridges' prose, which is admirable. Everything he wrote has in it something melodious or otherwise memorable. Though in its natural amplitude it may sometimes be thought to study nobility rather than convenience, it is a true expression of its writer, and closes always manfully with its theme. I would name more particularly his three biographies of Dolben, Canon Dixon and Henry Bradley, for he was an excellent memoirist; and also his well-known and still authoritative essay on Keats. It is the novelty of that essay that it is the criticism of a craftsman: most criticisms of such poets as Keats being only a mild and far-off raving. The usual kind of criticism would have been of no help to Keats and therefore of little interest. But he would have found technical pleasure in the method of the critic on hearing plainly that of the three short narrative poems *Isabella* is 'the worst executed'; that *The Eve of St Agnes* 'is well done throughout', and that *Lamia* 'is not all equally well written'. Keats and Bridges, one can see, would have understood each other. Bridges was aware of the innovation and defended himself in his concluding paragraph: 'If my criticism should seem sometimes harsh, that is, I believe, due to its being given in plain terms, a manner which I prefer, because by obliging the writer to say definitely what he means, it makes his mistakes easy to point out, and in this way the true business of criticism may be advanced.'

There is very good writing in the essay and in particular this fine passage:

'The song of the nightingale is, to the hearer, full of assertion, promise, and cheerful expectancy, and of pleading and tender passionate overflowing in long drawn-out notes, interspersed with plenty of playfulness and conscious exhibitions of musical skill. Whatever pain or sorrow may be expressed by it, it is idealised—that is, it is not the sorrow of a sufferer, but the perfect expression of sorrow by an artist, who must have felt, but is not feeling; and the ecstasy of the nightingale is stronger than its sorrow......'

He had written in his own *Nightingales*:

Beautiful must be the mountains whence ye come,
And bright in the fruitful valleys the streams, wherefrom
     Ye learn your song:
Where are those starry woods? O might I wander there,
Among the flowers, which in that heavenly air
     Bloom the year long!

Nay, barren are those mountains and spent the streams:
Our song is the voice of desire, that haunts our dreams,
     A throe of the heart,
Whose pining visions dim, forbidden hopes profound,
No dying cadence nor long sigh can sound,
     For all our art.

Alone, aloud in the raptured ear of men
We pour our dark nocturnal secret; and then,
     As night is withdrawn
From these sweet-springing meads and bursting boughs
     of May,
Dream, while the innumerable choir of day
     Welcome the dawn.

The memoirs offer more various browsing in all modes: as this on Dolben's father: 'As he did not ride to the Pytchley, he had such a reputation as a scholar will get in a hunting district.' Or on his mother: 'Mrs Dolben was a fine example of one of the best types of English culture...: such a paramount harmony of the feminine qualities as makes men think women their superiors.' Or on some early sacramental verse of Dolben's: 'The reading of these poems makes one see why schoolmasters wish their boys to play games.' On Dixon's painting: 'There exists...an easel-picture by him; this, hanging on the wall, might pass at a distance for one of the coloured prints published by the Arundel Society; if you go near, it reveals, indeed, a faith that should remove mountains, but also a very impressive view of the mountains which no faith can remove.' On Dixon as a curate, invariably misunderstood by his vicar and the congregation: 'We have now to think of Dixon as a curate in London: a most unusual curate. Unfortunately the idea of unlikeness to other curates gives no positive picture....But if his congregation had known him better they would have understood him less.' Dixon particularly tempted him, he loved him so much: 'Like his father he was a clerical smoker indoors, and, I think valued the use of tobacco too much to count it a luxury. His pipe lay on his writing-table in careless brotherhood with his old quill pens.'

Here I offer you three longer passages, as I do not know a better way of inviting you to read the memoirs:

'Happiness cannot be measured nor even described, but its conditions at least seemed here complete.

In one of the loveliest cities of the world—for almost all that may now hinder Oxford from holding her title is the work of the last fifty years—in a university whose antiquity and slumbering pre-eminence encourage her scholars to consider themselves the *élite* of the nation, there stood apart a company of enthusiastic spirits, in the flourish and flower of their youth, united in an ideal conspiracy to reform society by means of beauty. In the frankest friendship that man can know, when its ecstasy seems eternal, and time only an unlimited opportunity for agreeable endeavour, before experience has sobered enterprise or thought has troubled faith, these young men devoted the intention and hope of their lives to the most congenial task that they could imagine. Their light-heartedness never questioned their wisdom, and to their self-confidence all appeared as easy as the prospect was pleasant. They inherited the devotion that had built their schools and temples, and regarding the beauty that had been handed down to their enjoyment as peculiarly their own, since they alone worthily loved and adored it, they aspired to enrol themselves in the same consecration and rekindle a torpid generation with the fire that burned in their souls.'

'The summer of that year was wet in the North, and the persistent rain delaying my start made me relinquish the western end of my ramble, so it was by train that I arrived one afternoon, and first saw Dixon awaiting me on the platform of How Mill station. Emotion graved the scene on my memory; a tallish, elderly figure, its litheness lost in a slight, scholarly stoop which gave to the shoulders an appearance of heaviness, wearing unimpeachable black cloth negligently, and a low-crowned clerical hat banded with twisted silk. His attitude and gait as he walked on the platform were those of a man who, through abstraction or indifference, is but half aware of his surroundings, and his attention to the train as he gazed along the carriages to discover me had that sort of awkwardness that comes from the body not expressing the intention of the mind. His face, I saw, was dark and solemn, and as he drew near I could see that the full lips gave it a tender expression, for the beard did not hide the mouth. Nothing further could be read, only the old mystery and melancholy of the earth, and that under the heavy black brows his eyes did their angelic service to the soul without distraction. His hearty welcome was in a voice that startled me with its sonority and depth; but in its convincing sincerity there was nothing expansive or avenant. He then became so silent that I half suspected him of common tactics, and was slow to interpret his silence as mere courtesy, which it was; indeed, he would never speak unless he were assured that he was not preventing another, a habit which made a singularly untrue disguise of his eager, ingenuous temper. However, as we approached the village it was his call to talk, and he set me wondering by his anxiety that I should admire the church. It was a dreary, modern stone building with roundheaded windows and a wide slate roof; the shrunken degradation of a tower stuck on to one end and the after-concession of a brick chancel at the other.......I suppose he loved it as the home of his ministry.'

'Those nights I remember better than the days, of which, however, some distinct pictures remain: one is of Dixon's favourite walk in a deep combe, where the trees grew thickly and a little stream flowed by the foundations of old Roman masonry; another is a game of lawn-tennis—it could have no other name, for only the implements of that game or their approximate substitutes were used. The scene after thirty years is undimmed; I am standing with Dixon and two ladies in the bright sunlight on a small plot of grass surrounded by high laurestinus bushes in full flower, and crossed by festoons of light netting. I am more spectator than player, lazily from time to time endeavouring to place a ball where Dixon might be likely to reach it, or mischievously screwing it in order to perplex him. He like a terrier after a rat, as if there were nothing else in the world, in such rapturous earnestness that I wonder we did not play oftener.'

This last passage recalls Robert Bridges' old aristocracy of body and careless ease at games.

I wish that I had time to speak of Mr Bridges' work for English speech, of his lifelong and ardent interest in whatever might preserve its nobility of utterance and the significance of its sounds. He feared, not without cause, as the English language spread and wandered about the earth, a loss of grip at the centre, and it was for this reason above all that he welcomed wireless. All the crafts that concerned language were of interest to him, whether the language were to be spoken, sung, or read: he studied types and scripts like any other branch of fine art.

He felt deeply the unity of literature, of Letters. The unity of the craft of letters is an affair of the household, and operates in depth from grammarian to poet. Grammarians or critics, editors or printers, lexicographers or *vates sacri*, they were all to him 'of that ilk', and if they vexed one another, as indeed they often do, it was a fault of temper. One of his closest and dearest friends was Dr Henry Bradley of the Oxford English Dictionary. The Poet Laureate writing poems, and Bridges inquiring into the nature of our speech, are seen on this view to be in fact the same person working in the same material. 'The builders of the crypts', says Mr Ker, speaking of the Middle Ages, 'were recognized and honoured by the masters of the pinnacles; the poets in their greatest freedom of invention were loyal to the grammarians and moralists, the historians and lexicographers upon whose work they built.' Of this breed and of this polity was Bridges.

I am still left with the feeling of our loss, however due to nature, of the great Englishman he was. No man was more steadily true to himself. His physical and mental beauty matched each other, and equipped him superbly for the life he chose. He was of noble and even heroic presence, and his careless outdoor strength and grace, growing more picturesque with age, expressed the colour and delicacy as well as the masculine humour and outspoken freedom of his mind. He was poet, scientist, philosopher, naturalist, musician, philologist, typographer, and country gentleman—a mixture of qualities that would have been surprising in another man, and probably ineffectual, but that in him achieved their harmony. He grew up, through the kindness of fortune, unwarped by the struggle of living, with none of the inevitable vices of a profession. He used the gifts of fortune responsibly, setting an example of high-minded devotion to all the arts of Beauty and to the spiritual advancement of mankind. Before he died he delivered in the *Testament of Beauty* his message of belief in the goodness of the human heart, and of faith in the religious foundation of human life.